BERNICE MYERS

SIDNEY RELLA
and the
Glass Sneaker

MACMILLAN PUBLISHING
COLLIER MACMILLAN

With special thanks to
Lucile Ogle

Macmillan Publishing Company
866 Third Avenue, New York, N.Y. 10022
Collier Macmillan Canada, Inc.
Printed in the United States of America
10 9 8 7 6 5 4

Library of Congress Cataloging in Publication Data
Myers, Bernice.
Sidney Rella and the glass sneaker.
Summary: Sidney Rella becomes a football player with
a little help from his fairy godfather.
1. Children's stories, American. [1. Football—
Fiction. 2. Fairies—Fiction] I. Title.
PZ7.M9817Si 1985   [E]   85-3044
ISBN 0-02-767790-7

1

Sidney Rella
was the youngest
of Mr. and Mrs. Rella's children.
Each morning,
his mother and father
would go off to work
in their small store.
Each afternoon,
his two brothers
would go off to
football practice
in the local park.

And each day,
after school,
Sidney was left to do
the chores.

"We all have our
jobs to do,"
his mother would say.

Today
his brothers
were trying out for
the town football team.
But when Sidney Rella
begged to go with them
they only laughed.

"You're too small
to play,
and besides,
who'd want you
on the team?"

Sidney Rella
wished more than
anything else in the world
he could play on the team.

"But how can I?
I always have
so much work to do."

A small person
hiding behind a bush
motioned to
Sidney Rella
to come closer.

"Pssst!"

"Sorry I couldn't
get here sooner,"
he said.
"I was helping a friend
get a poor girl ready
to go to a prince's ball.
Boy, did she have
two ugly sisters!
And I mean ugly!"

"Spring is our
busiest season for
wishing,
what with all the
school exams,
football games,
stock market losses...."

"Now what was it
you were wishing for?
Oh, yes.
A new milking machine."

"*No!* I wasn't!
I was wishing I could
try out
for the football team!
But I have so much
work
I'll never finish in time."

The small man
waved his wand.

There was a sudden flash.

When Sidney
opened his eyes
the porch was swept,
the floors were swept,
the dishes were washed
and the dog was
half asleep.

"Hey,
   are you Superman?"
Sidney Rella asked.

"I'm your fairy godfather.
I'm here to make sure
that you go to the ball—
I mean the football tryouts.
So go!"

But Sidney Rella
didn't
move.

"I have no uniform."

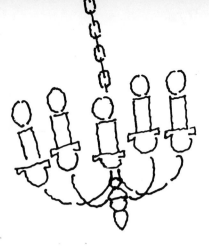

"That's easy to fix.
Bring me a tomato,
a pineapple
and a pear,"
the small man said.
And with a
wave
of his wand…
…the fruit was changed
into a beautiful uniform.

"This isn't a
football uniform!"
Sidney Rella complained.

"You're right!
I should have used
a carrot
instead of a pear.
Next time....

Make sure
you're home by
six o'clock,
or your clothes will
disappear
off your back."

2

Sidney Rella
was home
long before six o'clock.
He was all excited.
His fairy godfather
was waiting for him.

"I made the team!"
Sidney shouted.

"Terrific!"
said his godfather.
He waved his wand,
and Sidney Rella
had on
his own clothes again.
Then his godfather
disappeared.

At dinner that night,
the two brothers
could only talk about
football practice
and the new player
who could run as fast
as the wind
and catch a football
as easily as breathing.

Sidney
quietly
ate his soup.

The following week,
after school,
Sidney Rella
was helping his brothers
put on their uniforms.
"Well,
today's the big game, kid.
Too bad
you won't be there."

No sooner
had they gone
than Sidney Rella's
fairy godfather
appeared.
First
he made sure
all the work
in the house
was done.

"Now,
   let's see what the book says
   for a football uniform.
   A large pumpkin and
   four mice ....
   No, that's for footmen
   and a golden carriage....
   Here it is—football uniform.
   I'll need a carrot
   and a tomato,
   and two bananas
   for your glass sneakers."

Sidney Rella
returned
with his arms full.

His godfather
waved his wand
and Sidney Rella
stood
fully dressed
in the most beautiful
sparkling
football uniform and…

"Glass sneakers!"

Again,
his fairy godfather warned him.

"Be sure to be home
by six o'clock,
or your beautiful
football uniform
will disappear."

At the ball field
the stands were full.
Sidney Rella
took his place
in the line-up.

Each time the football
was passed to him,
he ran for a touchdown.

During the last minute
of play
the clock in the tower
struck *six*!
Sidney ran with the ball
for a final touchdown…

…and kept
right on running
till he reached home.

At dinner,
his brothers could only talk
about the game
and the mysterious
player
who had won the trophy
for their town.
"In his underwear, no less...."

"The coach is going
from house to house now
looking for the player
whose foot fits
the sneaker,"
a brother said.

When the coach arrived
at the Rella house
the sneaker didn't fit
either
of Sidney's brothers.

As the coach
was about to leave,
he saw
Sidney Rella
hiding behind a chair.

"How about you,
young man?"

"Oh, don't bother
with him,"
said one brother.

"He can't play football
or even catch,"
said the other.

But the coach insisted.
"I must try the sneaker
on everybody."

Sidney Rella
tried on the glass sneaker.
His foot slid right into it.
It also matched his other sneaker.

The coach invited Sidney Rella
to attend a special dinner
that very evening
where the mayor presented him
with a gold trophy.

Sidney Rella
grew up to be
one of the best
football players
in the country.

He went on to law school
and became a famous judge.

And then president
of a large corporation
that manufactures
laces for footballs.